Conversations with God

Conversations with God

You Heard My Cry

SHERONNA QUININE

Conversations with God: You Heard My Cry

ISBN 979-8-218-24502-3

Copyright © 2023 by Sheronna Quinine

Published by:

Noahs Ark Publishing Service
8549 Wilshire Blvd., Suite 1442
Beverly Hills, CA 90211
www.noahsarkpublishing.com

Edited by Carolyn Billups
Graphic Design by Christopher C. White
Interior Design by Andrea Reider

Printed in the United States of America © 2023 All rights reserved. No part of this book may be reproduced or copied in any form without written permission from the author.

TABLE OF CONTENTS

Introduction	1
Chapter One: A Safe Space	5
Chapter Two: Meeting Isaac	15
Chapter Three: Turning to God	23
Chapter Four: The Dark Period	31
Chapter Five: Thanks, for Not Answering My Prayers	39
Chapter Six: Who Do You Take God As?	49
Chapter Seven: Documenting Conversations	59
Chapter Eight: Image in My Sleep	71
Chapter Nine: Conversations with Healing	75

INTRODUCTION

MY WALK AND TALK WITH GOD

I often tell people, "I know how to pray dangerous prayers." It's one thing to talk to God, but quite another for Him to answer you.

I started talking to God as a little girl because I felt safe and believed He would not share our secrets.

While growing up in church, I witnessed many miracles and was fascinated watching people get healed, delivered, and set free.

During that time, I decided I wanted God to bless me with the gift of laying hands, praying for people, and watching God perform miracles.

Talking to God gave me comfort as a child. Our conversations were random at first. I often talked to Him while walking to the park. There was a park in West Covina, California where I would spend a lot of time sitting on a hill talking to God about everything. I shared everything with Him back then, just in case He was listening. This is how my journey of walking and talking with God began.

We talk everyday and He answers me audibly, through others, or in my mind. During my teenage years, God began speaking to me through His actions. What I mean by *actions* is, that whatever I prayed for happened.

As in most important relationships, I had good and bad talks with God. In the dark season of our relationship I cried, rebelled, and even cursed Him. On the other hand, I developed a solid trust and a great sense of peace, while also falling in love with Him.

Conversations with God provides practical and supernatural evidence that God hears and answers your prayers. I hope my story inspires you to start your own conversation journey with God or helps you as you continue your journey.

Childhood home in South Central Los Angeles, California
(photo by Zillow)

Chapter One

SAFE SPACE

The Early Years

My name is Sheronna Quinine. I was born at Martin Luther King, Jr. Community Hospital in Los Angeles, California. As soon as my father laid eyes on me, he gave me the nickname "Coco." When asked how he came up with that name, he insisted it was because I was a "chocolate" baby. From the hospital, I arrived at our family home at 1226 East 67th Street in South Central Los Angeles. This is where I grew up and spent my primary years as a child.

Our house was located directly across the street from my grandparents. My father was born and lived there until he met and married my nineteen-year-old mother. My mother was born and raised in Compton, California.

Shortly after my parents were married, they decided to start a family. My father wanted sons. They had four children. I am the youngest of two older sisters with one younger brother. Once my father had a son, my parents stopped having children. We lived in a small house with a dog and a yard full of roosters and chickens.

During the week, our parents spent most of the day working while our grandparents, watched over us. They made sure we were fed throughout the day, made it home from school safely, and remained safe until our parents returned home in the evening.

Spending Time with Grandparents

I enjoyed spending time with our grandparents the most because my grandmother often walked us to Franklin D. Roosevelt Park to swim and participate in recreational activities. Spending time with our grandmother also allowed us to play with other kids who lived on the same street as long as we remained safe and within her sight. She was very protective and did not allow us to refer to anyone as our "friend," as she insisted people were not to be trusted. According to my grandmother, we didn't have any friends.

My grandfather, "Gramps," was my favorite person. He loved to share historical memories about his upbringing and often quoted "The Good Lord" or "The Good Book" when teaching us right from wrong. He was flattered when I went to his church, Second Baptist Church, in Los Angeles. This was not often since my family and I were members of another church in Watts called Greater Wayside Church of God in Christ.

My grandfather also collected coins: quarters, dimes, nickels, and pennies. He stored them in small glass jars and gifted them to us for good behavior. I was always excited to receive a jar full of coins from him because it meant I would have plenty of money to spend at the ice cream truck. The sound of the ice cream truck could be heard several blocks away from my home. At seven years old I'd contemplate running to that truck full of goodies. I could hardly wait for it to arrive so I could buy candy, chips, and ice cream and do it all over again the next day.

The neighborhood seemed perfect. Besides the daily treats from the ice cream truck, I gained two best friends, Iesha, and Nicole. They lived on the same street several houses down the block. I liked hanging around them, and admired their freedom. It didn't seem as though they had as many rules and restrictions in their homes as we did.

For instance, in our home, our father was very strict. There were rules we had to follow. The girls had chores and were required to thoroughly clean the house before our parents made it home from work in the evening. Upon his arrival from work, my father sat in his recliner and called upon me and my sisters, one by one, "Rita, Vena and Coco!" We quickly stopped whatever we were doing to run and stand in his presence and respond to his requests. This often consisted of giving him the remote to the television, preparing his root beer float, and removing his socks and shoes. I would then smile and ask, "Daddy do you love me?" to which he would respond with these questions, "Do you have a roof over your head, food to eat, and clothes on your back?" That response was the extent of any love or affection we received in our home.

That's why having grandparents across the street, friends in the neighborhood, and attending Miramonte Elementary School in South Central was great. They served as a great escape and distraction from our life at home.

Elementary School in South Central

Although the school was within walking distance of our home, my parents dropped us off at school before going to work each morning. School was fun, and I enjoyed participating in festivities such as making my own costume with colorful tissue paper for Cinco De Mayo, learning to speak Spanish, and assisting the teacher with correcting math and spelling assignments. I also loved the pizza that was served for school lunches. My favorite time of the day was recess and physical education. I couldn't wait to compete against my friends in a game of handball and tetherball.

For the most part, things appeared to be going well outside the home, until my parents came home from work one day and decided we were moving to a new house in Compton, California. I was deeply saddened by the news of leaving my grandparents and friends behind, and even the small house that could hardly accommodate our growing family. I didn't know what to expect with the sudden transition to a new community, but at least I was able to remain at Miramonte Elementary through the end of the school year.

There was little to no communication in our household. So I was unclear as to why we were leaving a neighborhood we grew to love and call home. However, my father reminded us, consistently and almost daily, that he worked hard to provide and give us a better life. He even required my mother to accompany him to work on a regular basis to witness his labor.

My father was a strong, tall, intimidating, and prideful man. He spoke to people with direct eye contact and authority and often commanded the attention of anyone he came in contact with. In fact, the boys in the neighborhood avoided me and my sisters. They insisted they knew of our father and purposely stayed away.

Aside from hard work, my father seemed to enjoy spending time outdoors. After all, he was raised by my grandparents who were from Hungerford, Texas, where fishing and hunting were their favorite hobbies as a family. He gained experience in just about any outdoor physical activity and maintained his family's tradition by taking us fishing and hunting for family vacations in the summer.

Family Moves to Compton

The transition to the house in Compton seemed to suit my father's personality well. Arriving at the new house on 124th Street felt like a culture shock. For one, the size of the new house more than doubled the size of our previous house. The extended driveway was long enough to accommodate my father's newly acquired boat and RV. The backyard had ample space to run laps with the dog, compete in a game of tetherball with my siblings, and swim in the pool that was later added in the summer. The house was located just three blocks away from my maternal grandparents, where my mother was raised in Compton, and it was closer to our church, Greater Wayside COGIC, in Watts. I was okay with living closer to the church, as attending church with our family several times a week was a major part of our weekly routine. As early as I can recall, I was a member since my parents joined as church members long before I was born.

I didn't mind the distance to our maternal grandparents' house because visiting them for meals and fellowship after church on Sundays was part of our weekly routine. I enjoyed spending time with our cousins, getting my hair styled by my Aunt Pam, and running to a nearby house for junk food just one block away from my grandparents' house. We referred to the house as the "candy house" since the family was selling snacks, pickles, chips, candy, and soda out of their garage. I was called the "runner" because I was the one who often gathered our coins, jotted down orders, and ran to the local candy house when the adults were occupied inside my grandparents' house. We played outdoors with our cousins throughout the day until it was time to go home in the evening.

Family and Church Life

The church environment where we attended was structured and ladened with rules. For instance, it was uncommon for women to wear pants or makeup in the church. Women didn't preach or sit amongst the men during church service. Instead, they could be found caring for small children during service or serving snacks and refreshments after Sunday school.

Church attendance and participation were required by my father. He was highly regarded as a preacher of the gospel and met with married couples for counseling services and reconciliation as part of his ministry. The men at the church appeared to admire his stylish suits, latest choice in cars, and unique style of preaching that seemed to stir the entire congregation into an emotional uproar of excitement. The women, on the other hand, remarked how it must feel to be married to a hard-working, handsome, and God-fearing man who provided for his family and took them to church on Sundays. The women assumed my mother was lucky to call my father her husband, as we shared stories and pictures of being dressed alike during summer vacations. The presentation of our "perfect" family was fitting to protect my father's image.

My father was a young preacher who took pride in what others thought about his reputation and required me and my siblings to sit perfectly still throughout the service. If we were disobedient and laughed or joked around during church service, we can certainly expect to be brutally disciplined once we returned home. If we were disruptive during service, we understood his language amongst his church peers. He would smile and quip, "I have a surprise for you when we get home," and we knew exactly what that meant. We were hopeful the ride home from church would take as long as possible.

We participated in the children's choir called, "The Sunshine Band." I will never forget the bright yellow and white uniforms we wore while singing. We also attended Sunday school and mid-week "Bible band," a class that tested our memory and knowledge of scriptures in the Bible. In the summer, we attended vacation Bible school whenever it was in session. Like the adults, we attended "24-hour shut-ins," which lasted throughout the day and night. We had to stay awake while church members prayed throughout the night. We also attended local plays about heaven and hell and watched videos about "the rapture," that somehow always seemed to consist of someone going to hell and being punished for their sins. I had a tremendous fear of God and hell as a child.

My father was one of many preachers who preached a great deal about fearing God, faith in God, and righteousness. I was fortunate, as a child, that I did not have to question God's existence, having witnessed countless miracles. I saw people getting healed and being delivered and set free from their afflictions right before my eyes. It was very common to see people come into our small church in wheelchairs or crutches and then be up running around the church by the end of service, rejoicing with excitement after receiving a miracle from God. Their wheelchairs and crutches were later mounted on the walls of the church as a testament to God's miraculous healing. It was also common to see people who were possessed by demons be set free from their bondage. I was fascinated when God answered prayers right before my eyes. Right then, I knew I wanted to pray for people and watch God do it all over again when I got older.

I learned early on God can answer prayers and perform miracles for anyone who, with faith, asked and believed. I witnessed His response to prayer through various preachers and members of the church. I knew I could turn to God if I needed Him, but also felt like I had to be on my best behavior and close to perfection. I heard more about hell, sin, holiness, and things that made God angry, more than I heard about His mercy, love, and compassion. I knew I was imperfect, but I admired God's power and often wondered if He was mad at me for my imperfections.

Church had a significant impact on my life. It helped to establish my spiritual foundation and infinite knowledge of God as well as reaffirm His existence in my life. I enjoyed going to church with my family. I liked the same version of my father that the church members seemed to enjoy—the one who faithfully took his family to church to experience the presence of God each week. Unbeknownst to the church members, I didn't want services to end because that meant going home to a house filled with dysfunction and every form of abuse.

Family Falls Apart

Consequently, my family began to grow apart. It seemed everything was a trigger causing my father to react in anger towards his family. He began to mention less about his faith and more about his dissatisfaction with everyone around him, including God. The man who was once filled with pride appeared to be losing control and struggling, only to see the foundation that took him years to establish slowly but surely, slipping away. He stopped going with us to church, started drinking alcohol, and abandoned his faith. After thirteen years of marriage, he and my mother came home one day and announced they were getting a divorce.

I looked at my mother to see her immediate reaction, and she appeared to be deeply saddened by the news. Now she had four small children to feed. Although she remained calm and non-responsive as she allowed the tears to roll from her bruised eyes, she was undeniably broken. Despite the circumstances, my mother kept taking us to church. Shortly after she and my father were divorced, he remarried a woman he started seeing when he and my mother were still married.

My oldest sibling was devastated about my parents' divorce, as she longed to have a close relationship with our father. But for me, their divorce meant freedom. I was somewhat relieved knowing that I no longer had to worry about going home to an unpredictable, dysfunctional, and abusive environment. I would be free from anxiety and intense stomach aches that persisted just from the thought of going home from church or school. The divorce didn't solve all of our concerns, as it resulted in financial instability for my mother. We eventually ended up switching schools and neighborhoods more times than I can count.

My mother finally landed a stable job at Countrywide Financial in Los Angeles. I was at least ten years old when she invited me to work one day. I recall looking through one of the windows while standing on one of the highest floors in the tall high-rise building. I imagined myself as a businesswoman—nicely dressed in business attire, reporting to an office with a briefcase in my hand. I partially smiled and thought within myself, "One day, I will grow up and be an important businesswoman." There was no doubt in my mind. I was a dreamer and took advantage of getting lost in my thoughts every chance I had, just to escape my reality.

My mother enjoyed her new job at Countrywide Financial, but she had to remove us from Miramonte Elementary, which I was very sad to leave. Things also grew increasingly tense between my mother and father after he learned about a new guy she was dating. My mother enrolled me in a new school called Raymond Avenue Elementary in Los Angeles to finish my final year in elementary.

My Last Year in Elementary School

I quickly adjusted to the transition to Raymond Avenue Elementary. I had the best fifth-grade teacher a child with a dysfunctional upbringing could hope for. Her name was Mrs. Davis. I was instantly called the "teacher's pet" because she selected me for everything—including correcting homework papers, writing her lectures on the board, and volunteering to do any additional tasks as her helper. She made me feel like I was special. Mrs. Davis was beautiful, caring, and kind. One day, she selected me to join her and her family on a trip to Disneyland.

I had the best time with Mrs. Davis and her daughter at Disneyland. Going into the submarine was the ultimate experience. We laughed, ate snacks, and played games. After we left Disneyland, Mrs. Davis invited me to her home. I had no idea what to expect. When we got there, I did not want to return home! I wanted to live with her forever! Her life appeared to be perfect. She was happy, smiled often, and made me feel like I was very special to her. She treated me like I was significant every day that I spent in her class.

I was glad to report to school each day, as I knew I could look forward to spending time with Mrs. Davis. I was even happier when I met my first crush named Ricky at the school. Ricky had bright and beautiful skin with light brown eyes and sandy brown, curly hair. We had an instant and mutual crush on each other, and wore matching shoes and outfits as often as possible. He was my first kiss, and the thought of our connection gave me butterflies in my stomach. I was confident we would be in each other's lives for years to come. Until one day, my mother came home from work and told us we were moving again. But this time, she insisted, we were moving far away to a new city and community in Rowland Heights, California.

I'd never heard of a city called Rowland Heights in California. My mother explained she heard about the city from her best friend, Kyle, who was also relocating to a new community in Rowland Heights. My mother said she wanted to give us a better life in a different environment. I was about twelve years old when we relocated to Rowland Heights.

Chapter Two

MEETING ISAAC

Moving to Rowland Heights

The transition from Los Angeles to Rowland Heights had to be the ultimate culture shock, as less than one percent of the population in Rowland Heights were African American at the time. We moved to an apartment building called Parkwood Apartments. They were located on Fullerton Road with nearby schools, shopping centers, a bowling alley, parks, and other recreational activities that were all within walking distance of our apartment building.

My mother enrolled me in the local middle school, Alvarado Intermediate School, where I was set to start the seventh grade. I was nervous about the transition to the middle school and wondered how long it would take to adjust to the new environment and meet new friends. But the adjustment to the new school didn't take as long as I anticipated, and I met a small group of friends, Bridgette, Duane, Germaine, and Billy within weeks of attending the new school. They were cool, trendy, stylish, and loved to dance to hip hop music. We instantly connected and started hanging around each other during and after school. Also, Billy lived in the same apartment complex as me.

After school, we walked to the local shopping centers, hung out at the bowling alley, or went swimming in the pool at the apartment complex while my mother was at work. She was occupied with working two jobs to support our family and couldn't really keep up with our whereabouts throughout the day. My father stopped coming around as often because he was spending time with his new wife and caring for her two sons. They eventually left Los Angeles and moved to Henderson, Nevada.

During this time, my mother was hardly at home, but we still had to follow her rules. This meant we had to maintain good grades in school, keep the house clean, adhere to a strict curfew, not date or have a boyfriend, and not allow friends to come inside the house especially if my mother was not at home. I was beginning to enjoy the minimal supervision with my mother rarely home to enforce the rules. My life in Rowland Heights was much better and completely different from the situation we left in Los Angeles.

I tried to follow my mother's rules as much as possible while maintaining good grades throughout elementary and middle school. My siblings and I managed our chores to ensure the house was clean before my mother came home from work in the evening. Then it came time to transition to high school. I was not as nervous about the shift to high school because I was able to keep the same group of friends I had in middle school.

Going to High School

The transition to high school was overwhelmingly exciting. There was a restaurant on campus called "The Jar," and students had the opportunity to work there as a server or cook. We had the option to leave campus for lunch, as long as we had written permission, and return to campus before the end of the lunch period. The football and basketball games were fun to attend as this often meant meeting other students from rival schools. There were Sadie Hawkins dances and popular groups such as the Black Student Union (BSU) and Associated Student Body (ASB) to keep students engaged and occupied with educational and physical activities.

As a freshman in high school, I absolutely loved it. I had the same core group of friends from middle school, and we hung out daily in the same area during lunchtime. Due to increased popularity, our group began to expand. By the time I transitioned to the tenth grade, the size of our group had more than tripled. This was largely because my friends were trend setters who were heavily influenced by hip hop culture, clothing, music, and dancing.

Meeting Isaac

One of the new group members was Isaac, who had recently relocated from Carson, California. He moved to Rowland Heights to live with his Aunt Nelma because his mother was occupied with working a job in San Pedro, California. Isaac seemed to fit right in with the group, and he and Billy instantly became best friends. Isaac and Billy were inseparable, and the high school girls admired the way both of them danced and dressed. They somehow managed to wear rare and unique clothing items that were hard to find in local stores.

Isaac was very charming to be around. He had hazel eyes with light brown hair and was one of the few members in our group who owned a vehicle. I liked his personality. He was extremely laid back, outgoing, and joked about any and everything. We were polar opposites, as I was more serious, uptight, and often worried about making good grades or getting in trouble at home. He had the freedom to hang out as late as he desired without a curfew. He also had the gift of talking his way out of any dilemma or consequence that always seemed to work in his favor.

We were close friends and became attracted to each other within a short period of time. Before I knew it, we started dating. I was sixteen and he was seventeen. We were inseparable. I allowed him to hang out at my house whenever my mother was away from home, or we sometimes hung out at his house, as he lived in a less restrictive setting. One day, he stopped by my house to pick up my older cousin. They were close friends and had plans to go see a movie. But shortly before they left for the movies, Isaac and I decided to go into a room where I unexpectedly lost my virginity.

I was shocked and surprised! I called my friend Bridgette to let her know I'd just lost my virginity. I was feeling anxious, nervous, and immediately feared what would happen if my mother found out I was no longer a virgin. My heart was filled with guilt and shame, and I had every intention on keeping the news from my mother. However, a mother's intuition is undeniable. She began monitoring my behavior as soon as she became aware of my relationship with Isaac.

One day, I came home from school, and my mother confronted me about a recent change in my attitude and demeanor. She also described the difference in my sleeping pattern and insisted I appeared to be increasingly tired and was taking frequent naps on the couch throughout the day.

She asked if I was still a virgin. I tried my best to be dismissive to avoid answering my mother's question. When I ultimately declined to provide her with a direct response, she told me to go to the doctor for a pregnancy test after school and not to return home without giving her the results.

I was furious with her! I didn't think I could possibly be pregnant since I'd just recently lost my virginity. However, I was young, naïve, and knew very little about intercourse. I convinced myself that the symptoms described by my mother only meant I was transitioning into a mature woman since I was no longer an innocent virgin.

I wanted to diffuse the situation with my mother. So I called my boyfriend Isaac and told him about the argument. I insisted he take me to the doctor for a pregnancy test after school so I can make peace with my mother.

Baby News

Upon arriving at the clinic, we remained calm and relaxed. I just wanted to take the pregnancy test to give my mother a sigh of relief that there was no way I could possibly be pregnant. I entered the medical office and requested the pregnancy test while Isaac patiently waited in the lobby. After several moments of waiting for the results, the doctor entered the exam room and said, "Well, the results are definitely positive."

I asked what he meant by "positive," and to clarify if he was suggesting he was positive I was *not* pregnant. I reminded him that I needed to take the test results home to my mother. The doctor simplified his response and replied, "The results are positive that you are indeed pregnant." I was shocked and remained in the exam room to process the doctor's response. The first thought that came to mind was the fear of sharing the results with my mother.

After sitting in the exam room processing the news, I returned to the lobby to share the results with Isaac. He was nervous and surprised by the positive pregnancy test, but insisted he was very excited to have a baby on the way.

During the ride home, Isaac and I wondered how to share the news with our parents. After all, our relationship was fairly new, and we were just teenagers. We barely had the opportunity to really know one another before bringing a life into this world. I knew my mother was going to be disappointed, but Isaac was not too concerned about his mother's reaction to the news.

I dreaded the ride home from the clinic. I couldn't picture how to tell my mother that her sixteen-year-old daughter, who was recently voted most likely to succeed by her peers and consistently made the honor roll, was now pregnant with a baby on the way. Unfortunately, I had no other choice but to return home, as requested, to face my mother. I was hopeful though that she would have forgotten about the argument by the time I made it home.

As soon as I arrived home, I shared the news about the pregnancy results with my mother. The heated argument seemed to pick right back up exactly where it left off before I left for school. The argument quickly escalated with my mother expressing her disappointment in my actions. She insisted I would end up dropping out of high school and reminded me of the barriers that came with the responsibility of having a child. We continued arguing back and forth until she raised her voice and told me to leave.

I was emotional and filled with anger and called Isaac to pick me up from my mother's house. I told him she asked me to leave during a heated argument. He arrived at her house within a matter of minutes, and I gathered all of my belongings and left.

Leaving Home

I moved in with Isaac and his mother on White Cloud Ct. in Chino Hills, California. It was very uncomfortable at first because I didn't have the skills or experience to live independently. I was sixteen years old and in the first trimester of my pregnancy. I didn't know how to cook, do laundry, pay bills, etc., and couldn't imagine making arrangements for daycare or learning to drive a vehicle for the first time.

Shortly after moving in with Isaac and his mother, we started to clash. Isaac and I had frequent disagreements about morals and values and conflicting views on how we wanted to raise our child. His mother and I didn't get along too well. She constantly intervened during our arguments and seemed to always side with her son. The two of them often laughed at me for living in their house and having nowhere else to go. But Isaac reminded me on numerous occasions that I could gladly "get the fu** out" any time, adding that my own mother didn't want me.

From the Frying Pan to the Fire

I worried about the arrival of our child, having left a dysfunctional home only to enter a dysfunctional relationship. I didn't want our child to have the same dysfunctional and abusive upbringing that we both experienced as children.

My heart was filled with pain, disappointment, anger, hatred, bitterness, resentment, and all sorts of emotions. I was beyond exhausted from being asked to leave. Although I wanted to leave, I couldn't think of anywhere else to go.

I tried to keep myself distracted with obligations at school. I was in my junior year of high school and wanted to maintain good grades to successfully complete the graduation requirements. But I had to rely on Isaac for a ride to school, and the ride consisted of insulting remarks and heated arguments about my lack of independence. I remained strong and defended myself against Isaac and his mother during these arguments, but I cried myself to sleep at night asking God to come to my rescue.

Praying While Pregnant

I wasn't sure if God would answer my prayer because I felt He may be mad at me for making so many mistakes. I doubted I was even worthy of His blessings but, in desperation, I still cried out to God just in case He was listening and decided to respond.

I had conversations with God throughout my pregnancy. I prayed about the arrival of our son, and asked God to allow him to be a healthy baby boy who would grow up to be a leader not a follower. I prayed that he would always have a spiritual foundation and a close relationship with God.

I continued going to school while anticipating the arrival of our child. Just two months after my seventeenth birthday, our baby, Isaac IV, was born. He was a beautiful, healthy eight-pound baby boy. I became instantly protective as his mother and loved him more than anything in this world. I was willing to risk my life to make sure his upbringing was nowhere close to what mine was.

CHAPTER THREE

TURNING TO GOD

Nowhere to Turn

I was at odds with a relationship that was failing and couldn't return home, as my mother and I were no longer on speaking terms. I needed and longed for a safe space.. My heart was broken in pieces and filled with pain, betrayal, and disappointment. It seemed nothing was working, so I turned to God with my troubles.

I turned to God to have a space where I could be vulnerable, share my secrets, and not have to be guarded or defensive in His presence. It was the one place where I could remove my pride and break down and cry without being teased or ridiculed for my feelings.

I started our conversations with more crying than talking and didn't always have the words to express my feelings. There were no expectations when turning to God for answers. I wasn't really sure where I stood with Him since He remained silent during our conversations. Aside from God's presence, I made every effort to hide my pain, as I didn't want our beautiful son to know I was hurting. Looking into his eyes I'd smile, while singing nursery rhymes from the book I made for him during my pregnancy. I danced and laughed to stir up his excitement hoping he was too young to notice the tears simultaneously running down my face.

I took him for walks to Shadow Oak Park, a local park in West

Covina, California. There I sat on top of a hill and talked to God about all of my feelings. I knew I could tell God everything and was confident it was a safe space to share.

I did more talking than listening. I sometimes questioned God about sending everyone else a friend, loved one, or significant other to talk to, but not sending anyone for me. I talked to Him about anything that came to mind, whether good, bad, or sad. I kept walking to the same park and sitting on the same hill to share my feelings since there was no one else to turn to but God.

I yearned to have love, joy, peace, and acceptance, but always seemed to be disappointed with the outcome. I tried to find it in others, and resented the fact that all I had was God. I had no idea He was all I needed. I also didn't realize I was searching for something that could not be found externally. It could only be found internally through an established relationship with God.

I somehow minimized God's role and presence in my life and continued to focus on acceptance from my natural mother, father, friends, or significant other. I perceived my relationship with God as a backup plan or last resort. I didn't realize I would've been spared a significant amount of heartache and pain had I considered turning to God first, as my primary source.

I wanted to be loved and accepted by others and, therefore, strived for perfection. I figured people wouldn't notice the brokenness, pain, and dysfunction if they were too busy being distracted by my accomplishments. I often felt like they would love me or treat me better if I presented a different version of myself; if I consumed myself with being a perfectionist and an overachiever just to be accepted by others.

Grassy hill at Shadow Oak Park in West Covina, California

I maintained my honor roll status throughout elementary school, middle school, and high school, and was determined to graduate with my high school diploma. I remembered my mother's words during the argument, that I would end up dropping out of high school. I decided to do everything within my power to finish my high school education and remained in school throughout my pregnancy and childbirth. I couldn't wait until the day my mother would see me walking down the aisle to receive my long-awaited high school diploma. I figured she would be very proud of me for not dropping out of school as she'd predicted.

Graduation Day

Graduation Day had finally arrived, and, like the other students, I was distracted during the ceremony. I kept looking into the crowd anticipating my mother's arrival with my ten-month-old son. He was too young to understand the purpose of the ceremony, but I still wanted him to see me graduate.

Shortly after their arrival, the weather changed, and it started to drizzle. Before I knew it, my mother stood up, gathered my son and his belongings, and left the graduation. I was later told it was due to the change in the weather.

It took a lot of effort to earn my high school diploma. My life had been challenging since childhood and became increasingly challenging as a teen mom. I just knew the accomplishment of receiving my high school diploma would result in a significant amount of praise, acceptance, or recognition from my mother. However, the celebratory moment that I had long anticipated never seemed to materialize. There was hardly a discussion or acknowledgment of the significance of my achievement beyond that moment.

Looking But Not Finding Acceptance

I didn't stop seeking validation from others when I didn't get the desired outcome after the graduation ceremony. I kept telling myself, if I had accomplished more, not only would my mother recognize me, but my father, friends, and significant other would also acknowledge and accept me.

I continued to search for acceptance outside of myself and my relationship with God. I wanted to seek approval from a natural person. And, if I didn't receive approval from my mother, I resorted to seeking approval through a relationship with a significant other.

I often talked to God about my journey of seeking approval and acceptance from others, even though I started talking to God less frequently. I kept asking God to send me a person to be there with me and for me. Although I was too young and immature to realize it, He had sent me Himself. I found that the more people disappointed me, the more I talked to God.

I was transparent with God and knew I could not deceive Him. He knew me more than I knew myself. I shared all of my vulnerable feelings with God because I was fully aware He knew I was broken.

I remember talking to God about self-hatred because I reached a place of pain that made me feel anger and hatred for anyone who disappointed me and let me down. I remember thinking, "If I am angry with hatred in my heart towards everyone else, I must have the same feelings of hatred for myself," and I did.

I struggled with self-love and therefore gave the responsibility of loving me to others. I didn't realize how much power I was giving to them. To me, God's love wasn't enough because I couldn't physically see Him. There were times when I cried out to God and didn't feel His presence. So, I kept resorting back to seeking validation and acceptance from others.

I just wanted to know how it felt to be loved by others. I couldn't imagine a hug or hearing "I love you," as those words were rare to non-existent in our home. I didn't recall ever feeling loved outside the home. Without a doubt I loved my son from the moment he was born because I was willing to sacrifice and protect him with all of my heart. But did not share the same feelings about myself.

I remember asking God to "love me extra" during difficult days of feeling unloved. I also asked God to help me love myself, similar to the way He loved me. I knew the love He had for me, by far, exceeded any feelings I had for myself.

I didn't hear an audible response from God. I was too busy consumed in conversations about my feelings, which left very little room for Him to respond. But thankfully He responded through His actions. It started with smaller actions. I would tell God when someone hurt my feelings and, all of a sudden, the person called me to apologize for their actions!

Dealing with Self Esteem

At eighteen years old, I turned to God for self-esteem. I began talking to God about my self-esteem because I started to believe the negative words that others said about me. I will never forget the moment I looked into the mirror and cried because I was called a "black monkey" on numerous occasions in my relationship. So much so that I no longer had the ability to see my natural face. Every time I looked in the mirror, I saw an image of a black monkey.

I cried out to God asking Him to help me look into the mirror and see myself the way He sees me. Looking in the mirror was challenging at first, but I wanted God to change the person I had seen in the mirror. I began asking God to help me see myself as beautiful, as God does not make anything "ugly." I then started to practice looking in the mirror while referring to myself as beautiful.

The words were hard to verbalize at first, even though I continued talking to God about the way I viewed myself. I would ask Him to give me a glimpse of the way He sees me. One day, I looked into the mirror and the image changed! I saw my natural chocolate face and believed it was beautiful.

I kept turning to God as a way to cope with my problems, even though I was fully aware I was far from being perfect. But, in God's presence, I did not have to pretend to be perfect. I was certain He would accept me if no one else did.

On days of feeling hopeless, I turned to God for hope. I would ask Him to give me hope and reminded Him that He is the God who can give hope to the hopeless.

In times of feeling inadequate and worthless, I turned to God and said to others, "I may be worthless, but to Him I am priceless." I told God there was no value that could be placed on my life for Him to give me away. I reminded God of what I meant to Him, in spite of feeling insignificant to others. I told God I believed if I was the only person who existed on earth, He would have still made the same sacrifice of His only begotten Son just for me.

When Presenting Your Best Self Is Not Enough

I kept turning to God, and His role in my life began to assume that of all others. He was nurturing when I needed a mother, protective when I needed a father, and I had the ability to confide in him when I needed a friend. Unlike others, He had the ability to assume multiple roles at the same time with perfection, and I didn't have to do anything to earn it.

When I turned to God, there was nothing I could offer. I had childhood trauma, emotional baggage, problematic friendships and relationships, and unlimited tears. I was not in any position to offer God anything in exchange for His love, support, acceptance, or protection, which is what I needed the most.

How often do we hear of people casting someone aside due to having "too much baggage," or "nothing they could possibly offer," in exchange for our time, resources, or attention. With God, is it the opposite. The less I had, the more vulnerable I became in his presence. He welcomed me with open arms to give me exactly what I needed each moment.

This explains why we try to hide our imperfections and present the "best versions" of ourselves to friends, family members, employers, or significant others. We are not certain if the person will accept the "good, bad, and ugly." We therefore choose to present the "good," which appears to be the safest way to seek and secure love, acceptance, and validation from man.

I turned to God when I realized He picked me up for the same reasons man cast me aside. In other words, all the reasons that disqualified me with man, were qualifiers to be rescued by God.

Chapter Four

THE DARK PERIOD

Frustration Builds Inside

As time went on, I became increasingly frustrated with my reality. It had been almost two years since I left home at sixteen, and at eighteen years old, life began to feel overwhelmingly unbearable. I reflected on the journey from childhood to present and became frustrated with the thought of everyone's role in my life.

I was losing patience, as things were no longer making sense. I was tired of fighting for a better life and asking God to rescue me. I was mentally and emotionally exhausted from not seeing a drastic or immediate change in my situation or circumstance. It didn't seem to matter how much I tried to make things better, as the instability of my living situation progressively went from bad to worse.

I wanted my own apartment, but it seemed impossible. I did have sufficient income to afford one on my own. I was earning $4.25 an hour working in the Aviation Department at Mount San Antonio College in Walnut, California. At the same time, I was pursuing my Associate Degree in Child Development. However, my living expenses by far exceeded my income. My son's daycare expenses alone were $3.75 an hour.

In addition to the daycare expense, I had other monetary obligations that left me depleted financially. I was also exhausted from leaving for work and school extremely early each morning, then arriving home very late at night by way of public transportation. The repetition of the tiresome and daily routine did not make me feel like progress was being made. It seemed as though God was taking too long to come to the rescue.

My New Friend

One day as I was leaving my class to walk towards the local bus stop, I was approached by one of my classmates who offered me a ride home. She insisted she was traveling home in the same direction. I was too exhausted to wait for the bus to arrive, so I accepted the offer. During our ride home, she talked about her faith in God, and told me about her church in Los Angeles, Evangelistic Church of God in Christ. She shared testimonies about God's presence in her life and invited me to join her for one of their church services.

I accepted the invitation to church as I was in dire need of an inspirational word. I was also happy about meeting a new friend, who appeared to be very pleasant and kind. The following Sunday she took me to her church, and the service was amazing! From that moment on, the friendship quickly grew. We talked on the phone on a daily basis, and she made me feel hopeful by sharing examples of what God was doing in her life.

I was happy we met because I desperately needed a new church and a new friend. She was not difficult to talk to and didn't seem to mind taking me to church every week. The friendship felt like a safe space to confide and share details about my past and present situation, and she seemed to be a good listener. However, the more I became vulnerable and shared details about my pain, the more she would boast about her situation. The dynamic of the friendship transitioned from feeling like she was sent by God to be a positive light and inspiration, to someone who took pride in my downfall.

The excitement of riding with her to church was wearing off as her attitude and behavior towards my son and I felt belittling. She appeared to be appeased by my brokenness while boasting about the abundance of material possessions—money, cars and property—she insisted were blessings from God.

At the time I was confused. I couldn't understand how God would continue to bless someone who was visibly arrogant and spiteful and appeared to enjoy kicking people while they were down. She boasted about what God was doing in her life each week, and I couldn't help but wonder if He had forgotten about me. I figured if He could bless someone with a wicked heart, He could surely remember me.

I wondered if I was doing something wrong to cause God to take so long to answer my prayers. I needed an immediate answer to my prayers to rescue me from my living situation, which was stagnant and turned upside down. I began to feel as though God had forgotten about me, and the ride to church was no longer helping me to feel better. It actually left me feeling depressed and worse. I stopped accepting her rides to church and returned to isolation. The experience with my ingenuine friend was causing increased humility within myself.

Where Are You God?

At that moment, I stopped asking God for help. I grew tired of waiting for Him to answer. It seemed as though everything I longed for existed in someone else's life. I couldn't help but notice affectionate parents with their children and wondered how it must have felt to receive affection from a parent. I also wondered how it must feel when someone has a supportive significant other or someone to call a genuine best friend.

I knew I had a safe space to turn in God. I considered Him to be my ally. I would never doubt His existence, but I desperately craved His presence. He appeared to be silent, although I know He was aware of my suffering. But I couldn't help wondering about His role in my trials. I needed to know He was listening to our talks and if He planned to do for me what He had done for others.

My religious upbringing caused me to wonder if I was in good standing with God. I wondered if He stopped listening to me a long time ago. I reflected on multiple mistakes I made throughout the years and wondered if I was worthy to expect anything from God. But where else could I turn?

I started to blame God for everything that went wrong in my life, including my poor decisions. I figured He was making me pay for all my mistakes. He must have wanted me to suffer since I was a heavily flawed sinner.

These ongoing conversations with God slowly transitioned into questions, and I had plenty. I asked why He was there for others but not for me. I asked if He remembered me or had forgotten about me. I asked why He allowed people to hurt me, and why He didn't send a person to comfort me.

It did not matter how consumed I was with a busy school and work schedule. I managed to find the time to walk and talk with God at the same park, sitting on the same hill, but no longer wanted to talk about getting rescued, as it did not appear to be a reasonable request. I was convinced life was not going to improve and no longer wanted to entertain the idea of a better season that supposedly lay ahead.

Questioning My Own Existence

I asked God, "What's the point in waking me up each day if there is no plan for improvement?" I went on to remind Him that my life was bad, and He did not send anyone to be there for me. I asked about the purpose of a life filled with pain. He remained silent.

I was no longer hopeful that He was going to bring me out of my situation. I pictured my request just bouncing off a wall. Waking up started to feel like torture, and my anger was drastically intensified. The number of unanswered questions narrowed down to one, and I was very clear, "Why, God, why did You allow me to see another day?"

I continued asking the same question, as I could no longer be hopeful, and my tears were drying up. Things were no longer making sense. If there was no meaning to life, other than a bed full of heartache and pain, what was the point in living?

My attitude towards life had diminished, and I could no longer envision my life in the short-term future. The more God woke me up each day, the more I questioned the purpose. I was fully aware that it was God who granted me permission to see another day.

I was in a dark space and fantasized about death. Life didn't seem to have much to offer. The only sign of hope was the love I had for my precious son. I loved him more than life itself, but I didn't feel adequate to be his mother. I couldn't give him the life he deserved because I was too young and unstable to meet his physical and emotional needs.

He deserved more. He didn't ask to come into a world with two young and dysfunctional parents who didn't have a clue about parenting. He was going to suffer for our poor choices, just like I had to suffer as a result of my parents' poor choices.

He was, by far, the greatest gift from God. I loved him deeply from the moment he was created in my womb. I wanted to be a perfect mother, but the vision I had of parenting during pregnancy did not align with my reality.

I was hopeful he was too young to recognize tears, though I did try to smile at him while I was crying. I tried to keep him occupied with activities, as I did not want him to carry my emotional pain. I tried to conceal as much pain as possible because I didn't want him to worry the way I did as a child. I wanted his life to be pure and innocent and desired to protect him from any form of abuse.

I wanted a place of our own to call home—an environment that was safe and secure. I wanted him to enjoy his childhood and not be forced to grow up too fast like I did as a child.

God's Silence is Deafening

But God was non-responsive and remained silent. I tried to explain that if I couldn't look forward to life, maybe death was the ultimate source of rescue. I continued to inquire about the purpose of waking up and wondered if God took pleasure in my humility. I wasn't sure if it bothered Him to see me hurting. I began to sound like a broken record talking to God about the same thing without any confirmation that He was listening.

God's silence made me question if I was talking to myself. I wasn't sure if He still wanted to hear from me, and He didn't give me any signs that He was still listening. So, I gave up trying and concluded life had dealt me a bad hand while others were fortunate to have a better outcome.

I wondered why God allowed me to experience such humility. He was there when my significant other teased me about running to God as my source of rescue while boasting about having more money and resources than me. I wanted God to intervene and prove him wrong, but He remained silent.

God witnessed my every bad and humiliating experience, yet He remained silent. The more I complained, the quieter He became. I couldn't seem to get His attention with positive or negative actions. While complaining, he no longer appeared to be moved by my tears, questions, or subliminal remarks. I reached a point where it didn't seem to matter what I said or did, as there was no sign or indication I had God's undivided attention.

I grew tired of His silence. I didn't receive a response when I talked about the pain or when I questioned His desire to wake me up each day. I loved God, but I was mad at Him for possibly abandoning me when I needed Him the most.

I wondered why He didn't allow anything to change. He had the power to pull me out of my living situation at any time if He desired. I kept talking to God because there was no other choice. He was really all I had. I took Him through my ups and downs during this difficult and emotional journey.

I shared every vulnerable emotion in detail and often pleaded, "Lord, you see the situation," to direct Him to things that caused me pain. I wanted reassurance that He witnessed my suffering. I wanted to give Him sufficient reasons to rescue me from the pain.

He showed me no signs of a better life. So maybe it wasn't worth living But God didn't respond to my questions or remarks. He didn't fall for my negative attitude, constant complaining and expressions of resentment toward others. Instead, He allowed my situation to remain the same.

As God remained silent, the arguments within my relationship continued escalating. They reminded me to "get out," even though I did not have the financial means to leave. I reached a place of desperation and could no longer tolerate a toxic and unhealthy relationship. But I was too embarrassed to call my mother to inquire about returning home.

My Petition and Promise to God

I decided to do something to shift my conversation and relationship with God. I stopped talking to Him about death and started talking about my life. I needed an immediate response to get me out of my living situation!

For the first time, I petitioned God at eighteen years old. I'd never formally petitioned God, especially with a promise to give Him something in return. I needed to try something different, as I was under tremendous pressure to leave as soon as possible.

I petitioned God while crying. I told Him if He opened a door and put me in a situation where I could be independent, I would surrender my soul and serve Him for the rest of my life. I wanted desperately to be in my own place without having to rely on anyone for anything.

This petition marked the first time I made a deal with God in exchange for surrendering my soul. I am unsure if I understood the magnitude of my promise, as I was desperate and willing to try anything I had not tried before. I knew God was my only way out because there was no way I could afford a place on my own.

CHAPTER FIVE

THANKS, FOR NOT ANSWERING MY PRAYER

Supernatural Miracle

I was at my son's grandmother's house when I petitioned God for my own apartment. I had no idea how He was going to respond. A supernatural miracle was necessary to accomplish the feat of getting my own apartment. I did not have any credit history or sufficient income to qualify, and the only way a door was going to open was with God's divine intervention.

After talking with Him about my request, I took a walk to an apartment complex on East Valley Blvd. in West Covina. I approached the apartment manager and requested an application for an apartment.

He asked my unit preference, and I insisted that a one-bedroom was sufficient. I wanted to secure the cheapest apartment that would allow me to have my own space. I took the application home, completed it to the best of my ability, and returned it to the apartment manager the following day.

Upon returning the application, I asked the apartment manager about the estimated timeline for approval. He stated they were at capacity with no upcoming vacancies, and the wait list would likely take at least a year.

I went home and wondered about the next steps. I couldn't imagine remaining in my current living situation for another year—it was no longer sustainable. I was also aware that my options were limited since my income was not sufficient to carry multiple rental options.

I kept talking to God about my living situation and within two weeks of submitting the application, I received a call back from the apartment manager. He informed me I was approved for the apartment. He added that they did not have any one-bedroom apartments available. So, they decided to rent me a two-bedroom apartment, which would be ready for occupancy within the next few weeks.

God Grants My Petition

I was completely shocked and filled with mixed emotions. For one, I remembered my petition to God and my promise to live for Him if he blessed me to live independently. I couldn't believe how quickly the move-in date was approaching. Secondly, I was scared. I had never lived independently and barely knew how to cook, drive, or even do laundry.

I was certain life was about to change but had no idea what was on the other side of these changes that were vastly approaching. One thing I knew for sure—God had answered my prayer. This was direct evidence He was listening and responded to my request.

I could not make this happen on my own. I did not have any credit history or a stable, sufficient income, and was advised there was a twelve-month wait list. Yet I was approved for a two-bedroom apartment within a matter of weeks.

When I petitioned God, I told Him if He opened the door, I would serve Him for the rest of my life. In that moment, God demonstrated His power and authority. It was clear to me that He placed a significant value on my soul, as I promised to surrender if He granted me this blessing.

It was confirmation to me that God really loved me and desired for me to have a life filled with love, joy, peace, and emotional and physical stability. It also made me feel like I was important to God, and He cared about my wellbeing. He wanted me to be in a quiet place where I could hear Him speak to me clearly. I was going to be in my own apartment where I could hear from Him and serve Him as promised.

A Place to Call My Own

Just two months after my eighteenth birthday, the date to move in had finally arrived. I was excited and anxious. I did not have a lot of furniture to move aside from a queen-size mattress, given to me by my son's grandmother, and my son's bedroom furniture.

I did not feel fully prepared for the move, but didn't realize at the time, that God was working behind the scenes. He was sorting out the details while I questioned if He was listening to our prior conversations. All I needed to do was allow God to lead me to the next steps, which I did.

The apartment was located next to a laundromat, fast food chain, a bus stop, and a church called Pillars of Faith. My son and I temporarily attended this church because I had no car. I was not concerned about living in a place that was going to be near empty of furnishings. I was extremely thankful for a place to call my own and not have to worry about being kicked out of someone else's place.

Self Discovery

Shortly after moving into my new apartment, I started on a journey of self-discovery. Aside from my role in everyone else's life, I discovered that I did not really know myself. I began decorating my apartment and learning about my preferences in food, music, spirituality, hobbies, and so on. I learned how to cook a variety of foods and often played classical music after reading. It was a great musical genre to stimulate brain development for babies and toddlers.

I made a list of goals outlining my educational, professional, and spiritual aspirations. One of the primary goals was to learn how to drive. The list also included my goals as a mother. I majored in Child Development to learn more about how children developed over time and to strengthen my parenting skills. I also wanted to take my son to engage in nearby recreational activities to foster his development.

I enjoyed being his mother and had goals to work hard to create and maintain a safe, stable, and nurturing environment for him. I took pride in decorating his bedroom, similar to a preschool environment. I loved singing to him using songs from the handmade nursery rhymes I created during pregnancy.

Aside from God, my son was the most important person in my life. He gave me a reason to continue to strive for a better life.

The role of a parent is the hardest yet most rewarding job in the world. But once I met my son, I couldn't imagine life without him. His life gave me purpose. I was fully aware it was impossible for me to be on this journey as a young mom without total reliance on God. My relationship with God has brought me through some of my toughest battles..

Admittedly, life didn't instantly change and become perfect after settling into my new apartment. I still suffered from the emotional pain of my life experiences. I was feeling overwhelmed by increased financial obligations that kept me in fear of something going wrong. But I kept sharing my feelings with God for comfort and support. I had assurance that He was going to take care of me. After all, He was the one who blessed me with the apartment.

Remembering My Promise to God

I remembered my promise to God that I would surrender and give Him my life if He opened a door. I kept talking to Him and walking my son to the church next door. God really had my attention when He answered with the new place. I was very grateful for the blessing, and it made me feel I could trust Him to take care of me and my son every step of the way.

I often talked to God about how I wanted my son's life to be. I wanted him to have choices about what he would do for a living, who he would marry, and where he would live. I talked to God about keeping him safe and close to me and always wanted him to have a close relationship with The Father. I wanted him to be a leader and have a positive impact on this world.

I also talked to God about my life and how thankful I was for allowing me to make it through a dark period. I didn't lose my mind or give up and leave this world. I didn't know He was listening with the intention of responding to our conversations.

I talked to God about the type of life I wanted, which included a close relationship with Him. Having freedom and resources to choose where I wanted to live and work was important. I wanted my life to be completely different from the way it started and had no idea He would respond in ways I had not imagined.

I thank God for holding my hand when I wanted to let go. He was teaching me to trust Him for the bigger things, like asking for an apartment. Or the smaller things like helping me have a better, positive day. I was learning to go to God for any and everything that came to mind.

For example, I received a utility bill in the mail for thirty dollars and didn't have the money to pay the bill. I asked God to make a way for the bill to be paid. Out of nowhere, I received multiple unexpected checks in the mail in thirty-dollar increments.

I knew it was directly related to my request. There was another time when I was hungry and didn't have money to buy food. My money was consumed with living expenses. One day, a friend came to class with a large container of Italian food. She insisted she wanted to be a blessing to her classmates because God had blessed her. This was one of many occasions I knew God was taking care of me.

God wanted me to trust Him with my life. The more I demonstrated relying on His daily provision, the more He responded to meeting my needs. I will never forget when I talked to Him about driving because I didn't know how to drive. I was consumed with fear because I was in several traumatic car accidents as a child. But I was tired of taking public transportation.

Public transportation was exhausting, not to mention the rainy days walking to and from the bus stop. So, I consulted with God about driving a car. I enrolled in driving school at age twenty-one and didn't get my driver's license until I was twenty-two. I asked God to bless me with transportation to get to work and school.

My First Car

Similar to getting my apartment, I knew I didn't have sufficient income or job stability to afford a car. I was barely paying my bills, but it didn't stop me from believing God for a car. Thankfully, I lived within walking distance of a used car dealership. One day, I decided to walk to the dealership to inquire about a used car.

I had to provide proof of my two part-time jobs. I worked as an Administrative Assistant and Child Development Aide. When I got to the used car lot, the salesperson approached me while I was in deep admiration of a car I wanted. I pointed to a jade green Honda Accord and told the salesperson I really liked the car, even though my intention was to purchase a cheaper vehicle. I pointed to an older car that appeared not to be in working condition. To my surprise, the salesperson told me to pick any car I wanted off the lot. She assured me I would leave a happy customer if I chose the car I wanted. She believed the monthly payments would be affordable so, I selected the jade-green Honda Accord.

I was overjoyed wondering how I would drive off the lot without any driving experience. Excitement doesn't adequately describe my feelings. I couldn't wait to leave the dealership to thank God for responding to my prayer again! At twenty-two years old, He blessed me with my first car. Not just any car, but the car I wanted!

God continued to hold my hand and navigate me through life. He didn't always give me what I wanted but gave me exactly what I needed to get through those uncertain moments. The Lord responded to me more times than I can count. I only promised Him one thing in return, my soul. I couldn't imagine the value of my soul for Him to take care of me in so many ways. All I had to do was continue surrendering to His will. God had a purpose and plan for my life. He wanted the best for me, yet I couldn't see my value the way He did. I often settled for less, but He intervened with His love for me. I learned to thank Him for prayers answered and unanswered.

Thank God for Unanswered Prayers

I recall a time when I begged God for an opportunity to work at Countrywide Home Loans. A friend had an uncle who worked as a Regional Vice President for Countrywide. Her uncle oversaw eight different branches throughout the country. His lifestyle was the American Dream. He owned multiple properties, took vacations with his beautiful family and their nanny, and had access to unlimited resources. He gave me the best news when he said he would connect me with a few hiring managers at various branches. I was beyond excited and knew this opportunity would be the ideal solution for the lifestyle I imagined. I begged God to open this door for me. I got all dressed up for the different interviews and was confident I would land a position with one of the hiring managers.

After several weeks passed and no callbacks from anyone, I felt very disappointed and questioned God. I didn't understand why the doors weren't opening. I thought the interviews went very well and knew the job would be perfect to provide a better life for me and my son. A year passed, and I was informed that several branches at Countrywide had closed. Many people lost their jobs. The realization God knew this was not the best opportunity for me became clear. He knew their doors would close and had insight into the future I couldn't see.

God was less concerned about my feelings being hurt than securing that job. He was more concerned about what was best for me and my future. This was one prayer I was thankful He did not answer.

I can't imagine how many times I would've been spared heartache had I gone to God concerning matters of the heart. Like choosing who to date or who I should allow in my space. I should have allowed Him to open and close doors that were best for me. God is aware of every area of our lives—the beginning, middle, and end of every situation.

I was so young and didn't trust God during that time. I often chose the wrong type of man because I didn't seek God's approval. As a result, when relationships went bad, I went to Him to heal the broken pieces.

Choosing friends was no different since I allowed friends to choose me. There were times I was aware of their character deficiencies that were detrimental to healthy friendships. I just wanted to be accepted. But these so-called "friendships" often resulted in heartache, disappointment, and betrayal when I allowed them to come into my life. So, I went to God to fix what was broken by others.

God loves us so much that He allows us to make our own decisions. God remains faithful in all of our bad decision-making. There was a time in my life when I contemplated dating a particular guy. I informed God I didn't want to waste my time dating the wrong person and asked Him to show me the person's character and give His approval or disapproval. The next day, while picking up food, I saw the guy holding hands with another woman. All I could do was smile and thank God for answering my prayer. God quickly revealed the man's character and spared me from another heartbreak.

God is aware of our true intentions and desires to spare us from situations that can result in heartache, pain, and disappointment. God will allow us to make good and bad decisions so we can learn to consult Him in all areas of our life. He loves us more than we could ever love ourselves.

Chapter Six

WHO DO YOU TAKE GOD AS?

"Who Do You Take God As?" is a question I will never forget. I was twenty-six years old and attending a weekly Bible class at New Gethsemane Church of God In Christ in Pomona, California. There was a teacher named Dr. Marshall who said, "God is whomever you take Him as. Who is God to you? Who do you take God as?" Those questions really strengthened my faith. I discovered God's sovereign ability to do anything I asked according to His will and plan for my life. I continued asking myself this question through various trials and seasons of victory.

I thought about when I asked God to heal or "rescue me". I had complete faith He was able to do anything I asked Him to do. I referenced His promises in His Word during our conversations. God was always faithful when responding to my prayers.

I also reflected on times my conversations with Him were filled with doubt, unbelief, worry, and anxiety. It felt as though God was silent, and I questioned if He was really listening.

I asked myself how I would feel if someone came to me in a time of need yet doubted my ability to come through on their behalf. How would you feel if someone didn't have faith in you? You would probably be less likely or unmotivated to help someone who didn't trust you. But thankfully, God did answer my prayers when my faith was not as strong as it is now.

I continued asking myself, "Who did I take God as?" The response to my prayers multiplied when I considered God for who He is to me. He is the final decision-maker, father, healer, provider, and protector of my life. God is my primary source, and everything else is a secondary resource.

I valued our relationship and wanted God to know how much I loved Him. I wanted to please Him in all of my ways, and it was no longer due to fear or a religious upbringing. My relationship with God was built on a foundation of unconditional love. He loved me when I didn't feel loveable.

When you love someone, you want to please them. You are willing to make sacrifices to make them happy. I felt this way about God because He loved me first, beyond my imagination. He treated me with such importance that I wanted to please Him in return by trying to make better choices. I pictured my sins breaking God's heart even though I didn't want to break His heart. Our relationship was too precious.

Unforgiveness

I didn't want anything to come between my connection with God. I wanted to continue to grow and mature both emotionally and spiritually. One day, I asked God to show me my own heart. He showed me a heart filled with unforgiveness hindering my spiritual growth and development journey. He was patient and waited until I was no longer fragile. A time when I was in a place of spiritual maturity where I could work on those areas that needed improvement.

When God showed me my heart filled with unforgiveness, I was instantly convicted and knew I had to drop my pride and forgive those who wronged me. I was eager to get to the next season in my relationship with God and not allow any obstacles to disrupt my spiritual path. God showed me that the posture of my heart was unpleasant. Even though His approach was gentle , He made it clear I needed to have mercy, just as He has mercy with me. He also showed me I'd hurt some of the same people who hurt me. I wasn't the perfect daughter, and can recall times when I was disobedient to my mother. I left emotional scars in heated arguments with my son's father. I had to forgive them like I wanted God to forgive me.

I understood I never had the right to harbor unforgiveness, forgave those who hurt me, and also reached out to seek forgiveness in return.

When I released unforgiveness, I immediately felt a sense of freedom. The weight I carried was lifted and God was proud of me. I kept attending weekly Bible classes at New Gethsemane Church and learned more about pleasing God. I started asking Him to help me love people the way He loves people. My compassion for others increased exponentially, as did my desire for others to have a close relationship with God.

The Prodigal Father Returns

I became passionate about praying for others and prayed that God would save my family. Nothing was impossible for God! I started praying for my father. He was once a strong man filled with faith but grew angry with God for how his life turned out.

I prayed that God would save his soul before he left this world. My father didn't come around too often, although I kept talking to God about him. One day, I called Daddy and invited him to church. To my surprise, he showed up at my door the following day in a black suit, ready for church!

We went to dinner after church and talked about childhood memories. We talked about going fishing and hunting, and he expressed gratitude for the invitation to church. He was happy to spend time with me and his grandson. We talked about the church service and his discussion with Dr. Marshall in the new members' class. He said Dr. Marshall told him he would be preaching again. I was grateful he was happy with the love and compassion he received from the church members. I believe Dr. Marshall spoke life into him.

Forgiving My Father

I was happy to extend Daddy an invitation to church. That invitation turned into ongoing time I was able to spend with him, and my son. My father came to my house every Friday, and we enjoyed our time together. We went to the beach on Saturdays to watch people fish and made each other laugh. I introduced him to new gospel music, local eateries, and he would always say, "Coco, I wanna be just like you." I must admit when I talked to God about saving my father, I felt my request was nearly impossible. My father had abandoned his faith for nearly twenty years, and to witness his spiritual revival was a dream come true. He was falling in love with God all over again. He finally reached a place where he was at peace with himself. He asked me and my family members to forgive him for everything he did wrong in our childhood. Most importantly, he asked for forgiveness for abandoning our family. I forgave my father and was happy to call him "daddy" again. He started calling himself my number-one fan. I felt like a lucky girl. God was my spiritual father, and my daddy returned as my natural father.

When I forgave my father, it no longer mattered that I didn't have the opportunity to enjoy our relationship as a child. I was in my late twenties when we bonded, and I was excited to experience the feeling of his presence. God enabled us to re-establish our relationship when I opened my heart to forgiveness. I wouldn't have prayed for my father's soul without an open heart.

My father admired my relationship with God. He told me he wanted to surrender everything and completely live for God. Because when he was not living for God, he gave the world everything. He wanted to do the same for God.

He kept rushing to church to get there on time. He loved to hear the choir sing and didn't want to miss anything in the service. It was impressive to see his memory of scriptures throughout the Bible.

I was in awe of God answering my prayer concerning my father. He finally had joy and peace—a peace he lacked for decades. He wanted me to be proud of him and often talked about the day he could celebrate giving me away at my wedding.

I laughed when he insisted he was looking forward to celebrating the day I married. He was so protective of me and said whoever landed me was a lucky guy. I knew he wanted to be a part of that special moment.

When God answered my prayer, it really demonstrated His ability to do anything I believed He could. It became clear God's willingness to answer my prayers had nothing to do with the magnitude of the prayer but everything to do with my faith in Him.

I adopted the slogan, "Who do I take God as?" God's presence in my life was undeniable. He carried me through every trial and allowed me to experience seasons of victory. Life has never been perfect, but I was unmoved by trials as long as He was with me and, I knew He was with me every step of the way.

Father and Daughter Time

My conversations with God gave me amazing favor. It kept a roof over my head for eleven years, and I remained in school until I completed my bachelor's degree in business management. I never imagined I would make it this far during my seasons of darkness. God gave me the strength to keep going until I finished my four-year business degree, and my father was present at my graduation. He was yelling out, "I see you Coco!" That moment was sealed as the highlight of my life.

I kept talking to God and asked Him to bless me with a stable job and increased income, especially since I had recently upgraded my education. I told God the employers had no idea the decision to hire me was not up to them. It was up to God. I reminded God that He was on the other side of the interview. If this was the door He had for me, they would not be able to deny me.

I interviewed for a position as liability adjuster at Farmers Insurance and got the job before my bachelor's degree was posted. There is no one outside of God whom I could credit for elevating my life. God was the only one I could turn to in my times of need. He answered not always according to my wants, but my needs.

I was imperfect, but God remained faithful. So, I continued turning to Him. My father continued joining me and my son in church. He witnessed a small portion of my journey with God, and I believe it restored his faith.

My father was excited about his future and appeared to have a zest for life again. One day after church, we went to a restaurant as part of our Sunday routine. He asked me to go inside the restaurant to have dinner. He said he wanted to stay in the car because he wasn't feeling well. He complained of a stomachache. I asked if he was sure he didn't want to have dinner with us. He continued to complain about discomfort in his stomach while encouraging me and my son to pick up dinner for ourselves. We got our dinner and returned to my apartment.

The Diagnosis

My dad returned to his home and sought a doctor's care the next day for his stomach pain. The doctor ran several tests that revealed he had stomach cancer. The cancer was spreading throughout his body, and the doctor informed Daddy he had less than two months to live.

My father called me and shared the news. He sounded calm and assured me he was going to be alright. He was a strong man. He went to chemo twice a week and continued attending weekly church services.

To my surprise, he appeared to be overly consumed with joy during the service. He danced in church and told me he wasn't concerned about the doctor's report. He said he knew where he was going and reassured me he was going home to be with the Lord.

I had conflicting feelings. I didn't understand why God was taking him since we just restored our relationship over the past four years. I was sad to know he was transitioning soon, and it became apparent that our future plans would never come to pass. My heart was broken as I began to watch my father lose his strength yet maintain his faith in God.

He was eventually placed in a hospice facility and could no longer join us for weekend church services. After church every week, my son and I would visit him at the hospice facility.

Called Home

He could no longer speak at this point of his illness. I asked him if he was tired and ready to go home to be with the Lord. He nodded yes. I asked if his soul was ready to be with the Lord, and he nodded once again. I prayed for his soul, and the next day or so, I received a call he passed away.

I was deeply hurt but not surprised about the news. Somehow the gratitude of God changing his heart before he transitioned superseded my sadness. I asked God to save my father, and He did. My father was a changed man who redeemed the time he lost. He restored his relationship with Christ before he separated from this world. I couldn't ask for a better outcome. God totally answered my prayer regarding my father.

He gave me peace and comfort while grieving the loss of my father. I was grateful for God's love and mercy in forgiving my father and changing his heart before taking him home. I was also grateful to share the experience with my father's last spiritual journey.

When God answered my prayer concerning my father, I knew it didn't matter how big or small my prayer request was as long as I maintained my faith.

I continued turning to God in every season of my life. He remained the same whether it was joy, sorrow, victory, career change, or relationships. God was a constant in my life.

I continued my conversations with God regarding my goals, dreams, and aspirations, and He continued opening doors I never imagined and closing doors for my protection.

He allowed me to continue excelling up the corporate ladder while attending college to further my education. I completed a Master of Arts in Management at thirty-four years old.

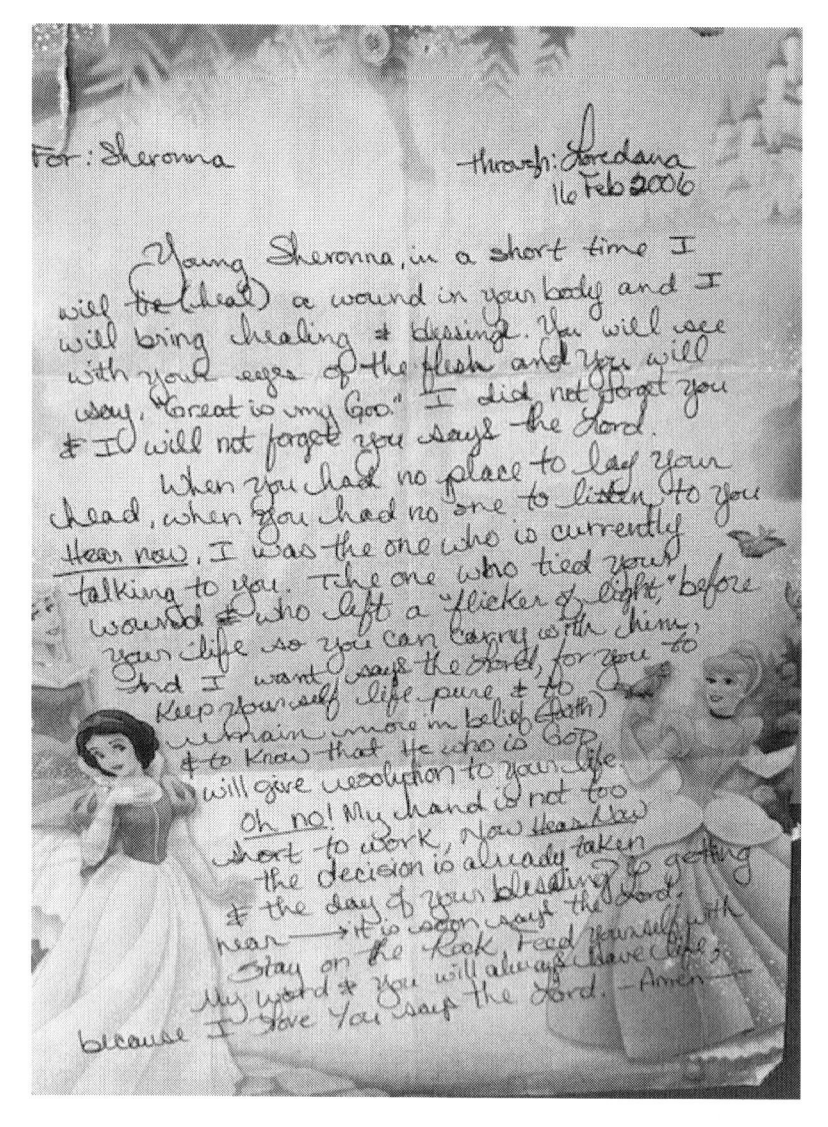

In February 2006, I attended a prayer meeting at a friend's house. During prayer, a young woman from Spain revealed a confirming word from the Lord. I knew this word was from God because the woman and I did not speak the same language, we never met, and the details in the letter were discussions between me and God only. The letter was translated to English, and I keep it posted on the wall of my prayer closet. It serves as a reminder that God is always listening, even when He appears to be silent.

Chapter Seven

DOCUMENTING CONVERSATIONS

On March 21st, 2018, these were the goals I wrote for myself:

- Become a Licensed Realtor
- Teach Online Courses:
  - Managing in Any Environment
  - Managing Career Transitions
- Listen to Podcasts
- Find My Place to Serve in Ministry
- Prayer Closet

I didn't realize the importance of documenting my dreams and goals at the time. I have since found my place to serve in ministry. Today, I am sharing that ministry with you, the ministry of writing.

In Habakkuk 2:2-3, the Lord instructs Habakkuk to, *"Write the vision, and make it plain on tablets, that he may run who reads it. For the vision is yet for an appointed time; but at the end it will speak, and it will not lie, though it tarries, wait for it, because it will surely come, it will not tarry."*

It's important to document meaningful moments on our life journey's. We memorialize our journey's through pictures, social media, apps, film, video sound recordings, etc., but there is nothing more important than documenting the words we receive from God.

My documented conversations with God provide a guided reference point for the rest of my life. Today, I have a loving relationship with my Confidant, Father, and Friend.

I would like to share with you the actual conversations I had with God. These conversations reflect a period of trials, pain, confusion, anger, and freedom.

January 03, 2021

Today is January 03, 2021, and I started my year the same way it ended. I desire to move forward and not backward in life. I start this journey in an effort to change my life and future. I want to grow and mature in many ways, and I pray that I will be consistent throughout the year.

January 04, 2021

Lord, I thank You for another day; thank You for my right mind, my health, my strength, provision, employment, and income. **Lord, I fast on behalf of my soul**. I want to live right; I want to live Holy and want You to be pleased with my life. I am an imperfect sinner and fall short by putting man and material gain before You. I repent and ask for forgiveness of all of my sins, spoken and unspoken. I pray that you will use me, and I will be obedient to Your Word. I lay aside every sin that easily besets me, discord, gossip, my job, disappointments, complaining, unforgiveness, and bitterness, and pray that this fast will change my life and draw me closer to You.

January 05, 2021

Lord, I fasted on January 05, 2021, for the sake of **spiritual growth**. While I am not satisfied with my behavior on yesterday and today, I pray that I will be consistent and never stop trying to live right. I ask that You help me make my **relationship with You** my priority and I will seek You and put You first above all things. Forgive me for all my known and unknown sins in Jesus' Name, Amen.

January 06, 2021

Lord, I pray blessings over my life and the lives of everyone connected to me. I pray that we would prosper and put You first and remain humble with our blessings. I pray for local employment that matches or exceeds my salary. I pray for successful businesses that generate more success than I would've ever imagined, and pray I will offer these blessings to You by paying my tithes and that these blessings will benefit the kingdom.

January 07, 2021

Lord, I fasted yesterday to **trust You enough to pay my tithes**, and You are the one who blesses me with or without the job. You are my provider and way-maker. Forgive me for not trusting You and being a robber, and I pray that I would be a blessing to the kingdom this year, more than I ever have.

January 08, 2021

Lord, I bring before You, Bobby, Isaac, and Jonathan. I pray for guidance, protection, and direction. I pray that you **save, set free, and deliver them from their sins**. Lord, Jonathan's life is in your hands. I pray that You would intervene and save his soul and keep and restore his mind. I pray that nothing in his life will happen outside of Your will. Favor in the courtroom, and I pray that he would be a light in prison. I pray that You would grow Isaac and Bobby with guidance and purpose and that they would be the men You created them to be, in Jesus' Name, Amen.

December 07, 2021

Lord, **I want to start a new routine**. I want to spend more time with God. I didn't know I would be in this situation as I sacrificed and worked to make it through escrow. I kept saying I didn't think I could make it through the next year, as the environment was bad for my health. **I want to start with gratitude**. Lord, I thank you that I have a place to live, for reconciliation with my son, comfort while going through the loss of my dog, and the means to pay my bills. While going through this journey, I am beginning to think about ideas. I want to create a journal. In order to create a journal, I need to practice for myself. I also want to finish my real estate license. I had faith that I would move into the house because I had a job that demonstrated I could make the payment. However, faith is tested when I don't see the means. My job ended, and I don't see the steps. But my Father is in control, and my future is up to Him. I am hurt, embarrassed, and disappointed, and want to go through this trial so God can be proud of me. Lord, on Tuesday, December 07, 2021, I am believing You to finish what was started in my journey to become a first-time homeowner. I begin this prayer by saying I believe in You to make a way on December 07, 2021, to remove any obstacle and allow the door to open for my new home. I understand this will happen according to Your will. The date this prayer was answered on…

December 11, 2021

Lord, **I went back to therapy yesterday.** Lately, I've been too discouraged to write…

January 07, 2022

I would like to share with you an oral conversation I had with God on January 6, 2022 while walking in the park. You can also scan the QR code below and listen to the conversation I had with God on YouTube.

> Okay Lord
> I'm here going on a walk
> today is January 6, 2022.
> just declaring and
> Testament of my faith
> God, I believe you I believe you're a God
> that can do anything but fail everything
> in my situation looks crazy
> I'm in escrow it's projected to close in
> March, I'm at this park in Moreno Valley
> right behind
> where they're building the house at
> and I just want you to know, Lord, that I
> love you, I trust you I'll take you at
> your word, and I believe you
> I thank you in advance for my house
> everything looks crazy I have to have

crazy faith, nothing in my life looks
like it's going to come to pass
I have no job
no income, I was wrongfully terminated
but Lord, you said vengeance is yours
and um
I thank you for peace
That Paul talked about how it's good
to be afflicted, I thank you that you
trusted me
during this trial that you will not lose
me you will never leave me nor forsake
me
and I thank you in advance
uh for how you're going to bring me out
Lord, you know even after you bless
me
I'm still gonna stick with you

DOCUMENTING CONVERSATIONS

My desire for a prayer closet was an entry in my journal on March 21, 2018, and it came to fruition exactly four years later, on March 21, 2022. I was seeking a designated and intimate space to have continued and ongoing conversations with God. Today, I continue to use this space to also feed my spirit through worship music, inspirational sermons, and documentation of my spiritual journey.

June 08, 2023

Lord, please do anything you want in this fast. Heavenly Father, the purpose of my fast includes spiritual growth, wisdom, clarity, guidance on writing my first book, deliverance, and whatever You want to do in me. Please change and purify my heart that I may do Your will and have healthy relationships to carry out Your will. I pray that You will help me to have discipline with my mind, flesh, ears, sight, and the words that I speak. I pray that I will grow in Your Word and focus on my relationship with You. The fast will include the following: Monday, 24-hour fast; Tuesday through Sunday will be without food through noon; no sweets or social media; and reduce calls without substance. I will not shop for anything outside of groceries. Food will be replaced with prayer and feeding my spirit with the Word.

June 09, 2023

Lord, I fasted through noon today, had a great prayer while taking a shower, and fed my spirit. I was emotional and didn't realize I need a lot of counseling for trust, trauma, and abandonment issues. I start counseling next Wednesday. While taking a shower, I was emotional thinking about the women who might benefit from my story and prayers. I will start back writing today. Laval asked me to complete chapter one this weekend. This fast has me emotional. Then I thought about the women whom my testimony would bless. I also want to write this book to be obedient to God's purpose and plan for my life.

June 10, 2023

Lord, it was a rough night. I had nightmares about someone cutting my hair. I was yelling and calling the person a "b**ch" multiple times when my son woke me up. Thankfully, I do not have a headache like

I did the day before. I pray that I will gain more strength each day. Guide my hand while I share my story. I pray for wisdom, guidance, obedience, and discipline to stay in this course to win. I am also excited about starting therapy next week.

June 12, 2023

Lord, today was the first time I fasted for twenty-four hours. I had a migraine headache and a difficult conversation with Laval throughout the night. I am feeling sad and discouraged today. I am overwhelmed and heavily burdened. I start counseling on Wednesday and am looking forward to it. I fed my spirit and prayed.

June 13, 2023

Lord, I fast on this day and am believing You will make me whole. I am feeling weak because yesterday was my first twenty-four-hour fast. I was told I am "flat" and not living but walking around dead. It was also said that I was insecure and always worried about others. Lord, I pray I will look to You for joy, love, and peace, not man. Help me draw closer to You. I pray that You heal, deliver, fill me where I am empty, and love me even when others find me unlovable.

June 14, 2023

Lord, thank You for this seventh day of my fast. Please give me what to share in this book. Allow the Holy Spirit to guide my hand. I want this book to impact millions around the world. That they might establish a relationship with you and know you will consider them perfect regardless of their imperfections. I start counseling today and pray that my life will change. I know it takes a special man to deal with me, but I am also a special woman. I am feeling stronger than

I did yesterday. I pray for the person you have prepared for me that they may have a blessed day. I pray I can be vulnerable with them and they will be open and receptive to constructive feedback and communication. I pray they will not have double standards and they will make me feel chosen out of all the women in the world.

June 15, 2023

Heavenly Father, I started counseling on June 14th, and the session went great. I shared my history of childhood trauma, trust, abandonment, and feeling inadequate. The counselor will help me retrain my brain, battle "emotional demons," and identify trigger points. He advised me to purchase a book "Cognitive Behavioral Therapy in 7 Weeks" about training the brain. He also told me to write three things I am grateful for on a daily basis, and I can list my stressors. But I pray I can give my stressors to You. Today, I am grateful for good health, Your love, and Your presence. Stressors to give to You: concerns about heavy work burden, lack of peace, and purpose. My purpose: grow in my knowledge of Your Word, build my competence and confidence, be a loving servant. I want to inspire others. I fast today on behalf of my thoughts and to retrain my thinking to be more like You.

June 20, 2023

Lord, I fast and pray that I will not be moved by things that take place around me, whether they are connected to me or not. I pray that You will do whatever needs to be done in me to live out Your purpose and plan for my life. I am grateful for God, Isaac, and my publisher. Thank you, I love You.

June 21, 2023

Lord, today is therapy, and I am feeling inadequate. It seems like my presence or contribution is always dismissed. I am believing You for total favor and victory in every area. The prior law firm is less than cooperative, and I pray the law firm and employer would be exposed and surrender, in Jesus' name. You will grant me favor and victory, just as You did with the house. I am grateful for a beautiful home, employment, and good health.

June 22, 2023

Lord, today I fast and pray for emotional healing. According to the therapist, we heal in three ways: spiritually, physically, and emotionally. Please heal me emotionally so I am no longer allowing people to take advantage of me for their love, acceptance, respect, or anything else. I pray that I will set healthy boundaries according to Your will. I am grateful for Your love, mercy, and forgiveness, Amen.

June 23, 2023

Lord, I fast today to turn from my wicked ways and die to self. I pray my life will be consumed with fulfilling my purpose. Remove my stubborn and self-centered fear, fear of rejection, worry, being hard on myself, etc. Help me to be the Godly woman You created me to be. I pray I will be quick to listen and slow to speak. I am grateful for my strength, gifts, and love for God. In Jesus' Name I pray, Amen.

June 25, 2023

Pastor Belle asked us to write down things to reconnect us to our passion for the next thirty days. This is the first day, and I desire to be reconnected to my passion for prayer.

June 26, 2023

Lord, please reconnect me to my passion for loving others. I pray I will see people the way You see them and love as though I've never been hurt. I pray I will demonstrate love, patience, kindness, compassion, and understanding. I am grateful You allowed my son to see twenty-nine years, is in good health, and has a relationship with You. I fast today, concerning my heart. Deliver me. I pray my heart will be pure. Give me the heart to serve, love, seek change, inspire, and teach. Change my heart how it needs to be to satisfy Your purpose and plan for my life.

June 29, 2023

Lord, I fast today for total surrender and trust in You. I ask that you reconnect me to my passion for seeking You and trusting You with every detail of my life. I am grateful for Your consistency in my life and grateful for my experience with You on this journey. I am thankful You have never given up on me.

July 01, 2023

Lord, I thank You for another day, and the weather is beautiful. I thank You for this journey I have been on with You and pray You will reconnect me to my passion for serving others for I am a servant. I am grateful for my book that will inspire millions to establish a relationship with You. I am grateful I still have the desire to seek You and that You love me with an everlasting love. I pray You will bless me with wisdom, enlarge my territory, and give me the desire to be obedient, in Jesus' Name, Amen.

Writing and sharing my conversations with God has provided me with a wealth of growth in my self-esteem, love, and inner peace. Thank you for allowing me to share my documented journey.

Chapter Eight

IMAGE IN MY SLEEP

A Spiritually Good Place

We will never reach a place on this journey where we become immune to trials, unforeseen situations, and circumstances. I thought I had reached a place of spiritual maturity since being on this journey with God through most seasons of my life but had no idea what was about to transpire next.

I thought I was in a good place spiritually in 2018. I had just left a friend's annual retreat in Big Bear, California, where I was one of the featured guest speakers conducting a workshop to inspire women about fasting, prayer, and perseverance.

I referenced the story of Jonah in the Bible. Jonah was instructed to preach repentance to the people of Nineveh. However, Jonah felt the people of Nineveh did not deserve God's forgiveness. In Jonah Chapter 1:3-17, Jonah flees on a ship that is cast into the sea and swallowed up by a whale because of his disobedience. He spent the next three days in the belly of a fish until he repented and asked God for deliverance. God demonstrates His mercy and compassion and returns Jonah to his rightful place. God gives Jonah another chance to fulfill his mission and execute God's instructions.

The women seemed to enjoy the workshop. One of the ladies asked if she could keep the lesson I prepared because it inspired her.

The retreat went well, and I was determined to return home with the same spiritual strength that was demonstrated during the retreat.

Battling Demonic Presence

I was unaware that I was headed for a demonic battle. I drove home, got settled, unpacked my belongings, had dinner, and went to bed. In the middle of the night, I was awakened by a huge dark presence that filled the room. I felt the presence of something dark, and its features were huge and disgusting. The spirit kept hissing at me like a serpent. The monstrous size of this being appeared to fill a large portion of my bed.

Moments later, I felt this large being trying to suffocate or strangle me. I began to pray loudly while gasping for air. I yelled, "The blood of Jesus!" and it hissed a few more times. I continued to pray loudly and commanded it to flee.

I woke up with a headache, and I was drained. I felt like I just finished an intense battle. I was puzzled and questioned myself. I wondered how this demonic being had access to my world.

I questioned if there was someone in my life who needed to be cut off. I'd recently been told someone around me was operating in witchcraft. I also pondered if something in my house needed to be thrown away or if I fully surrendered my life to God. Were there areas I hadn't fully surrendered to God or traits I still wanted to be part of my identity?

I was unsure why I had this experience but didn't share it with anyone because I wondered if something was wrong with me. I knew I could pray and cast this darkness out of my presence. I witnessed demons being cast out of people growing up. I never imagined encountering one in my own personal experience, and I was hopeful the experience would not happen again.

The day quickly turned to night. I was exhausted from the battle through the night. There was also a part of me that was hesitant about going to sleep because I couldn't help but wonder if the demonic being would reappear. I was too exhausted to stay awake long.

I remained awake until my body was depleted of energy and retired to my room for bed. The demonic being re-appeared in the middle of the night with the hissing sound. I looked up, and the monstrous being appeared to fill my room like a large black cloud of smoke. It hovered over me as if to strangle me again. I prayed loudly, and every time I yelled, "The blood of Jesus!" it trembled and shrunk, then dissipated. The more I yelled "Jesus!" it shrunk and dissipated. It disappeared after a few more hissing sounds.

Winning the Battle

On the third night, I had the exact same experience. I contemplated calling a friend, even though I wondered what she would think of me. I know demonic activities and witchcraft are not popular topics of discussion but, I wanted to enlist support from a strong spiritual friend to ensure the tormenting experience would not continue to disturb my peace.

I decided to call my friend Carlotta who shared my experience with another friend named Cynthia. Cynthia told Carlotta she would contact me shortly for prayer. I received a call back from Cynthia and her husband, who asked me what was going on. I shared my experiences regarding the demonic presence during my sleep. While they prayed for me, her husband said the demonic being was exiting out of the window during our prayer session. Cynthia's husband assured me I would never have another encounter with the demonic being again. Thank God, I never had another encounter with a demonic presence again.

Chapter Nine

CONVERSATIONS WITH HEALING

Conversations with God have been life-changing in ways I could never imagine. It has given me a safe and secure space to seek God for comfort and guidance during some of the most enduring seasons of my life.

During these turbulent seasons, I could feel God's presence, as He allowed me to experience answered prayers in unconventional ways.

07/04/23: Today, I am committed to maintaining a close relationship with God through a lifelong journey of emotional healing. I am also committed to utilizing my experiences to encourage and inspire others in similar situations to do the same.

My relationship with God lacked consistency throughout the years. I turned to God when I needed to be rescued. I didn't always keep my promises when He answered my prayers. I sometimes lacked consistency in my commitment to Him if the answer to my prayer was not what I envisioned or had in mind. I spent less time with God than I used to because I was too busy idolizing the blessings that manifested from answered prayers.

I mastered turning to God but was inconsistent in my commitment to our relationship, but God never changed. I may have moved from one location to another, one job to another, or one relationship to another. Even from one church to another, but God remained constant in my life.

He remained faithful and trustworthy. As I said, God has never failed me yet. It's amazing how God can deliver on His promises time after time. Yet we continue asking Him to prove Himself to us over and over again.

I've personally witnessed answered prayers and God's manifestation of supernatural miracles in my life. All of my worldly accomplishments can't compare to what God has done and is doing in my life. And all God requires is submission and obedience to His will.

I've learned that a relationship has to be nurtured because anything we feed will grow. I must therefore maintain a hunger and commitment to my relationship with God by spending time in His presence daily. Today, I continue reading His word, feeding my spirit through sermons and fellowship with other believers.

I am also committed to a lifelong journey of emotional healing through therapy and people who inspire me to journal, exercise, and stay connected to friends and loved ones.

I am sharing the most intimate details of my life and spiritual journey with an expectation to motivate and encourage others to seek a personal relationship with God. I know He is waiting for you with unconditional love.

God doesn't give up on you, so I encourage you to keep going and never give up on yourself. All you need is a conversation with God.

You might be saying to yourself, *"How can I get started on my own Conversation Journal with God?"* Well, maybe you can get started with this model letter that I created for you:

CONVERSATIONS WITH HEALING

Date: _____
Time: _____

Dear God,

_____

_____

_____

_____

_____

_____

_____

_____

_____

Thank you for listening. I look forward to hearing back from you.

Name _____

You can fill in the body portion of the letter with your own words to God.

Congratulations on your documented journaling with God!

For Speaking Engagements, Book Signings, Appearances, and Interviews

Contact:
Sheronna Quinine

Email:
mysheronnainquiries@gmail.com

YouTube:
@MySheronnaQ

Made in the USA
Columbia, SC
04 September 2023